Best Of Bastard

Hilarious Vulgar Adult Swear Word

Coloring Book For Release Stress

Violin Villa

Happy Coloring!

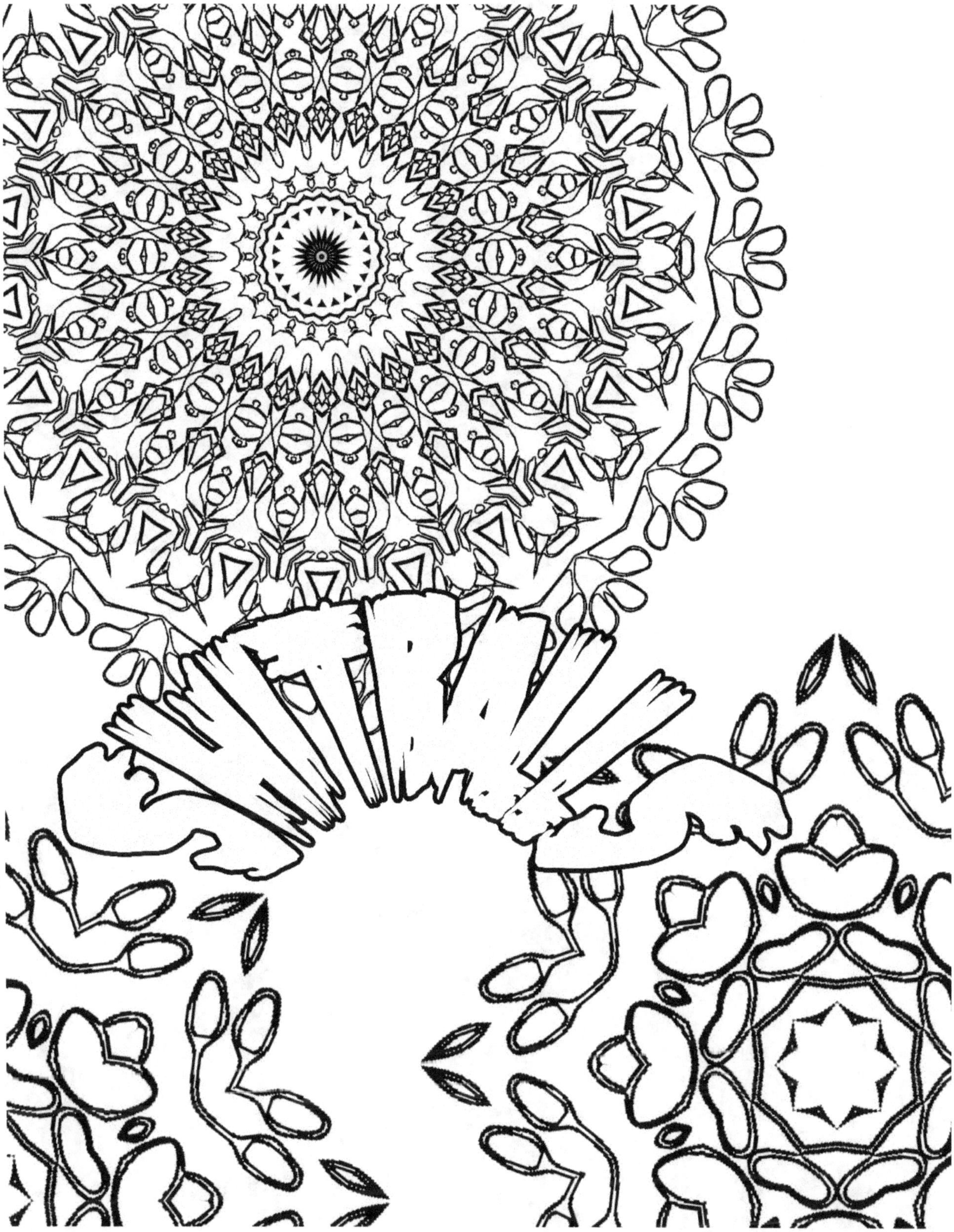

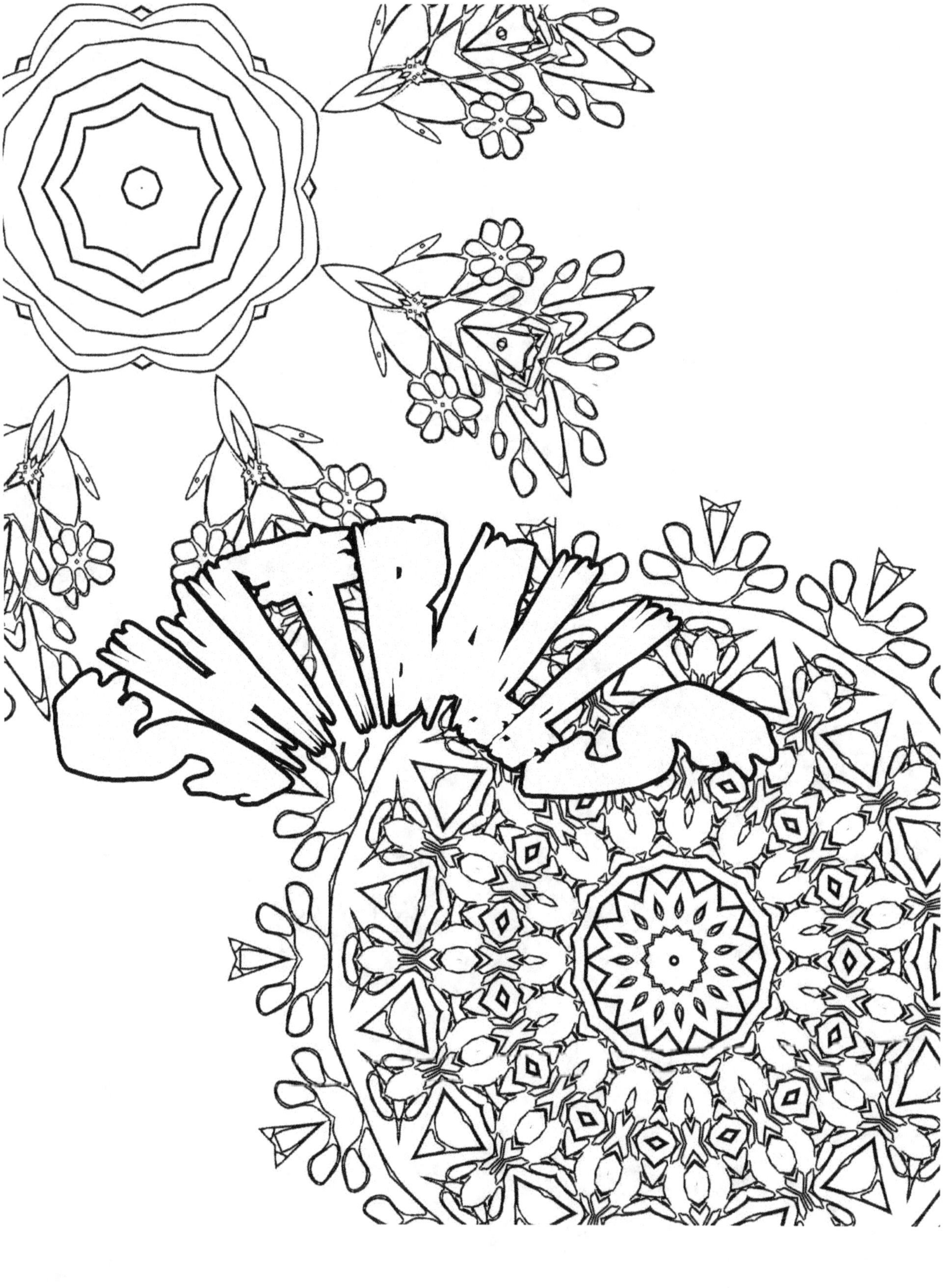

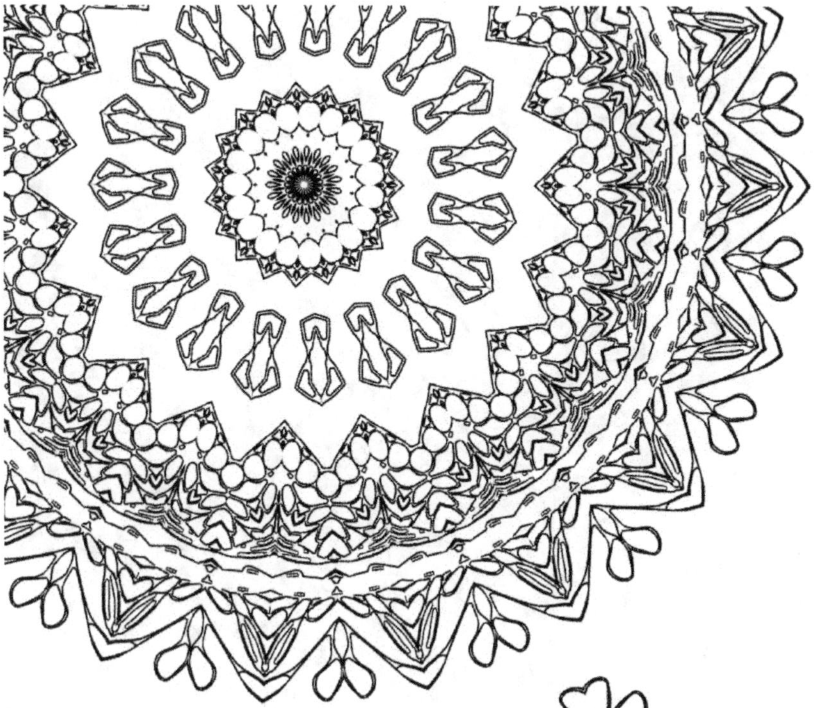

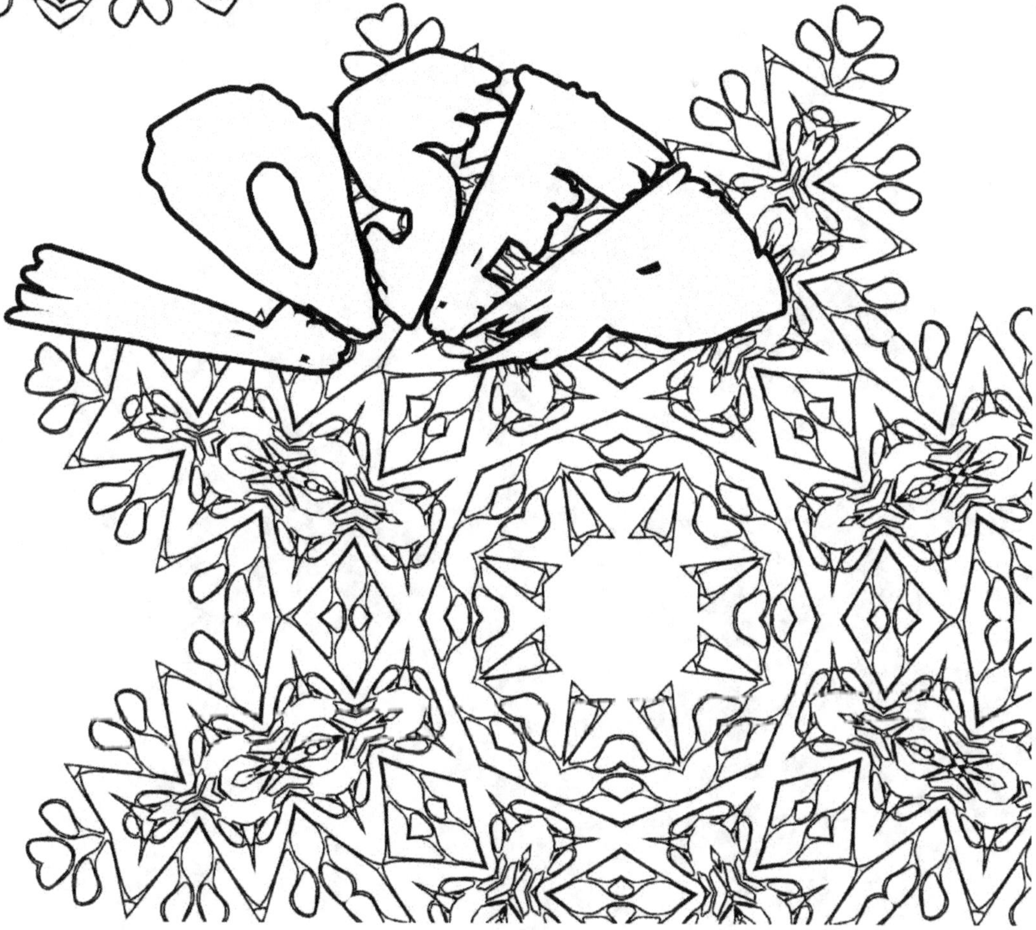

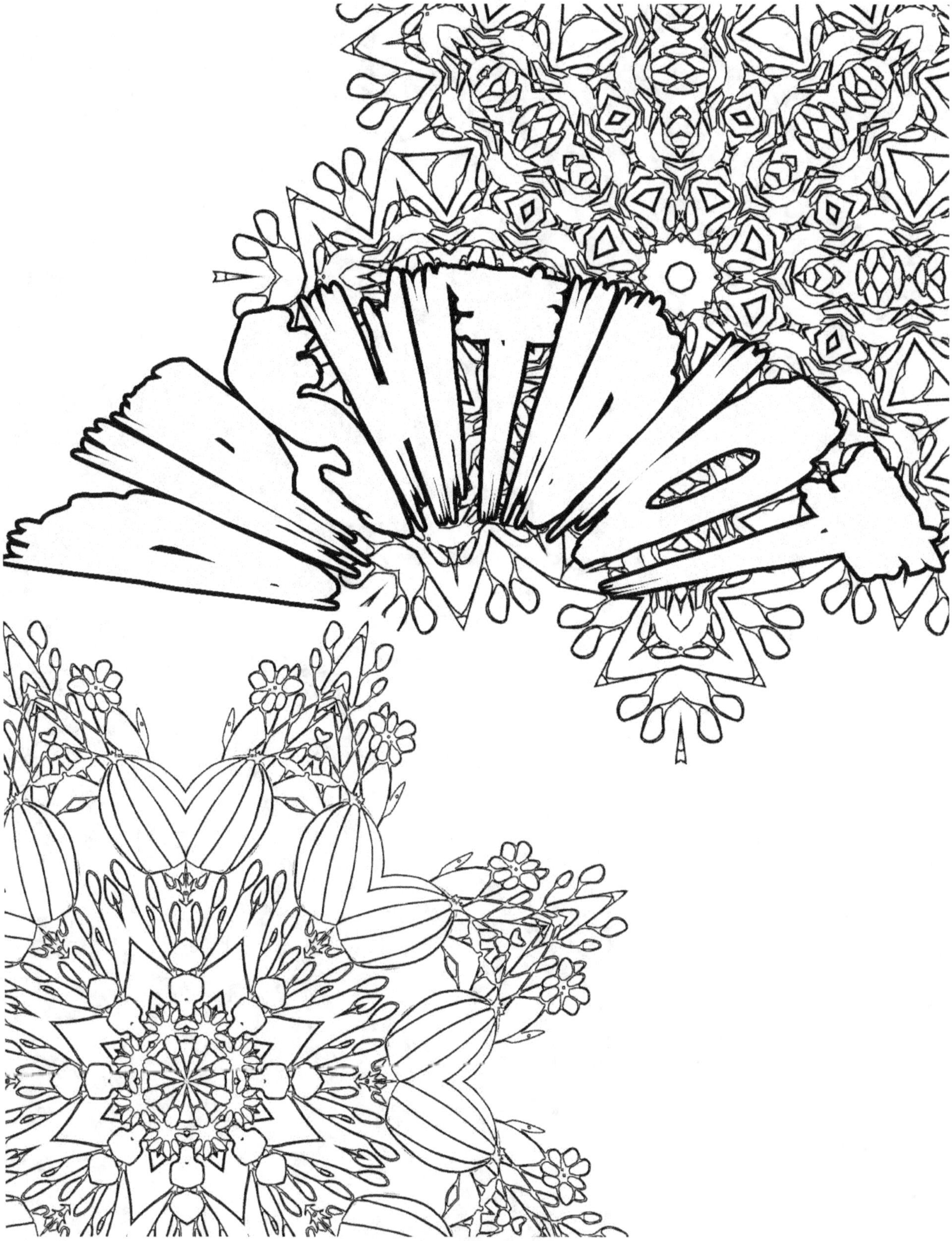

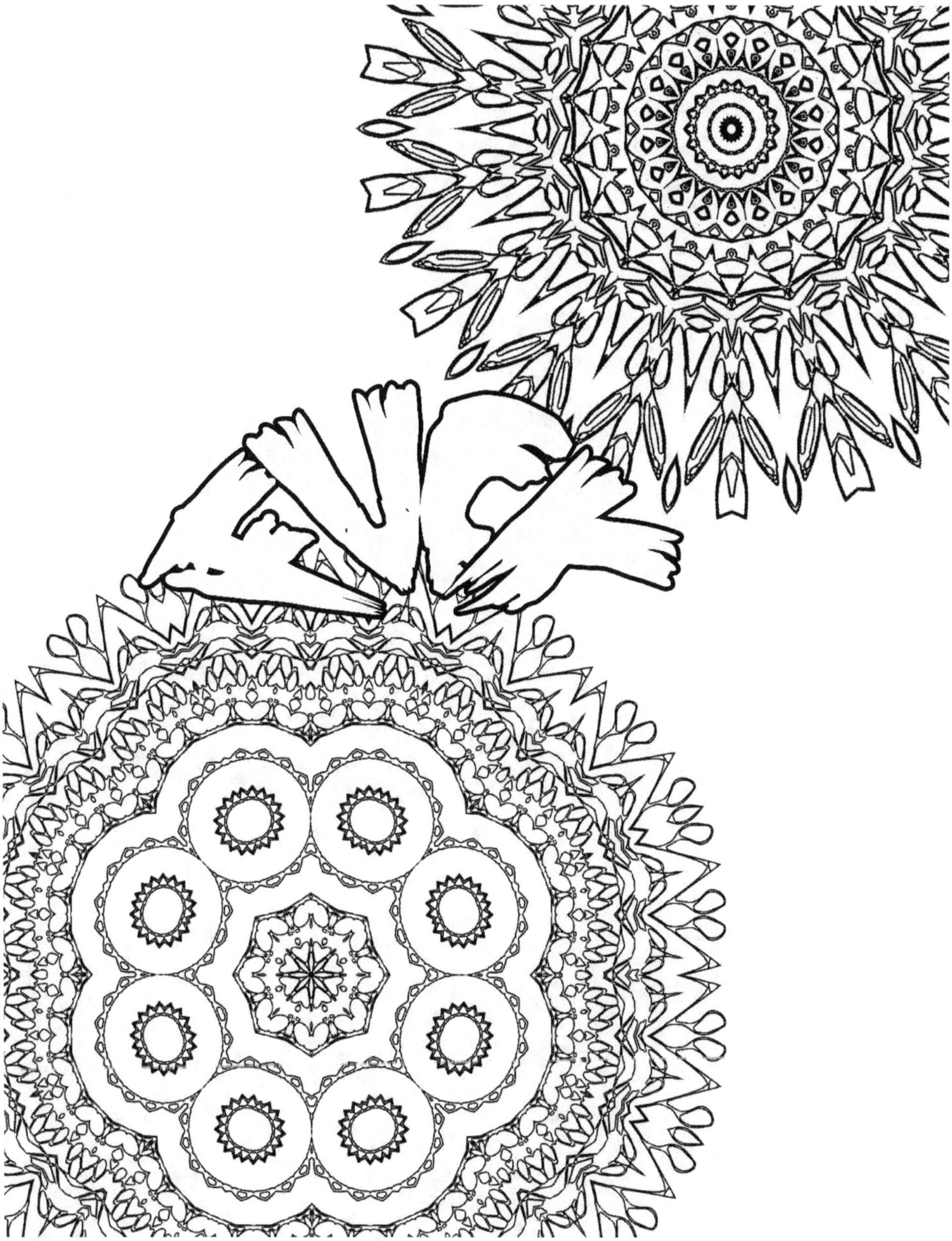

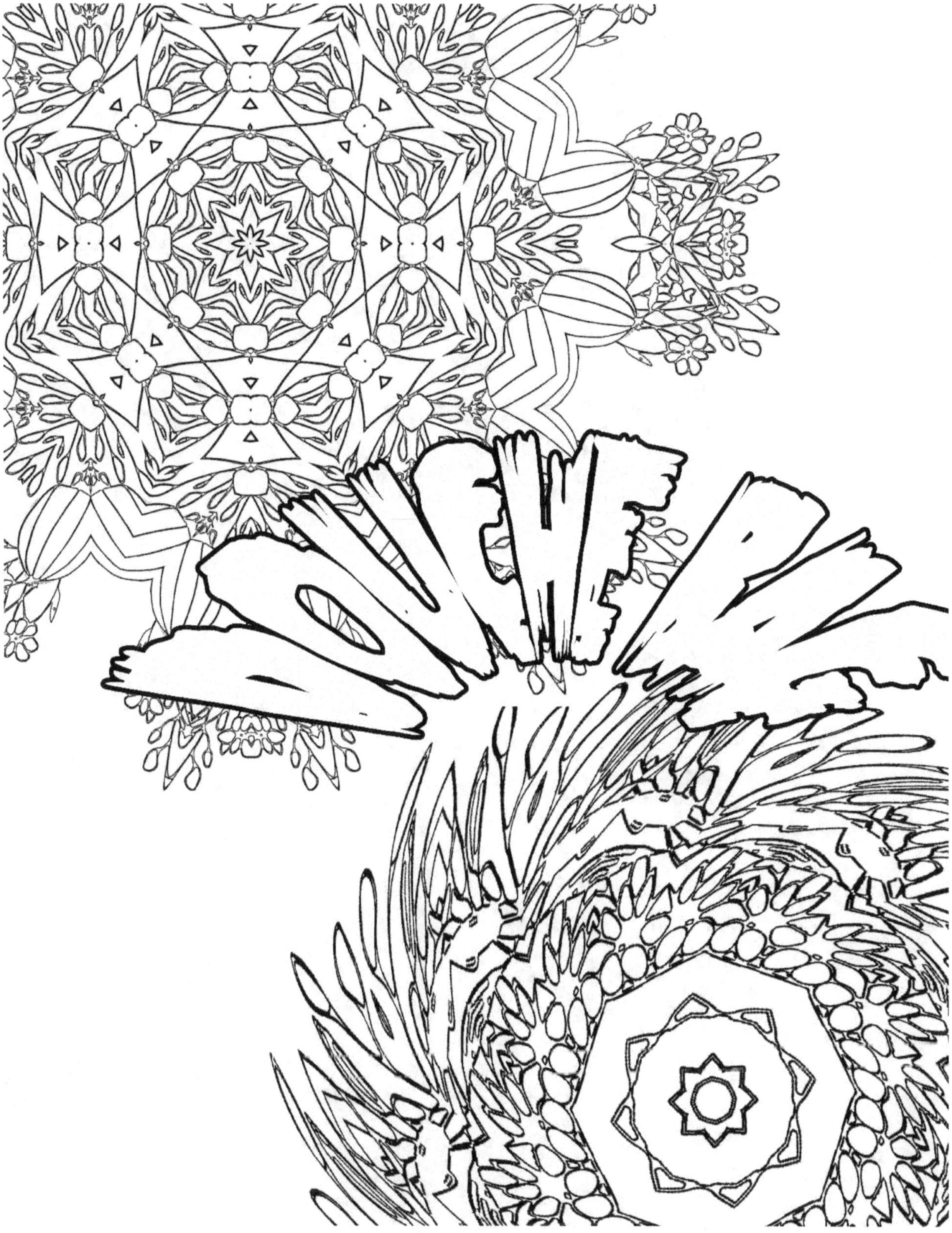

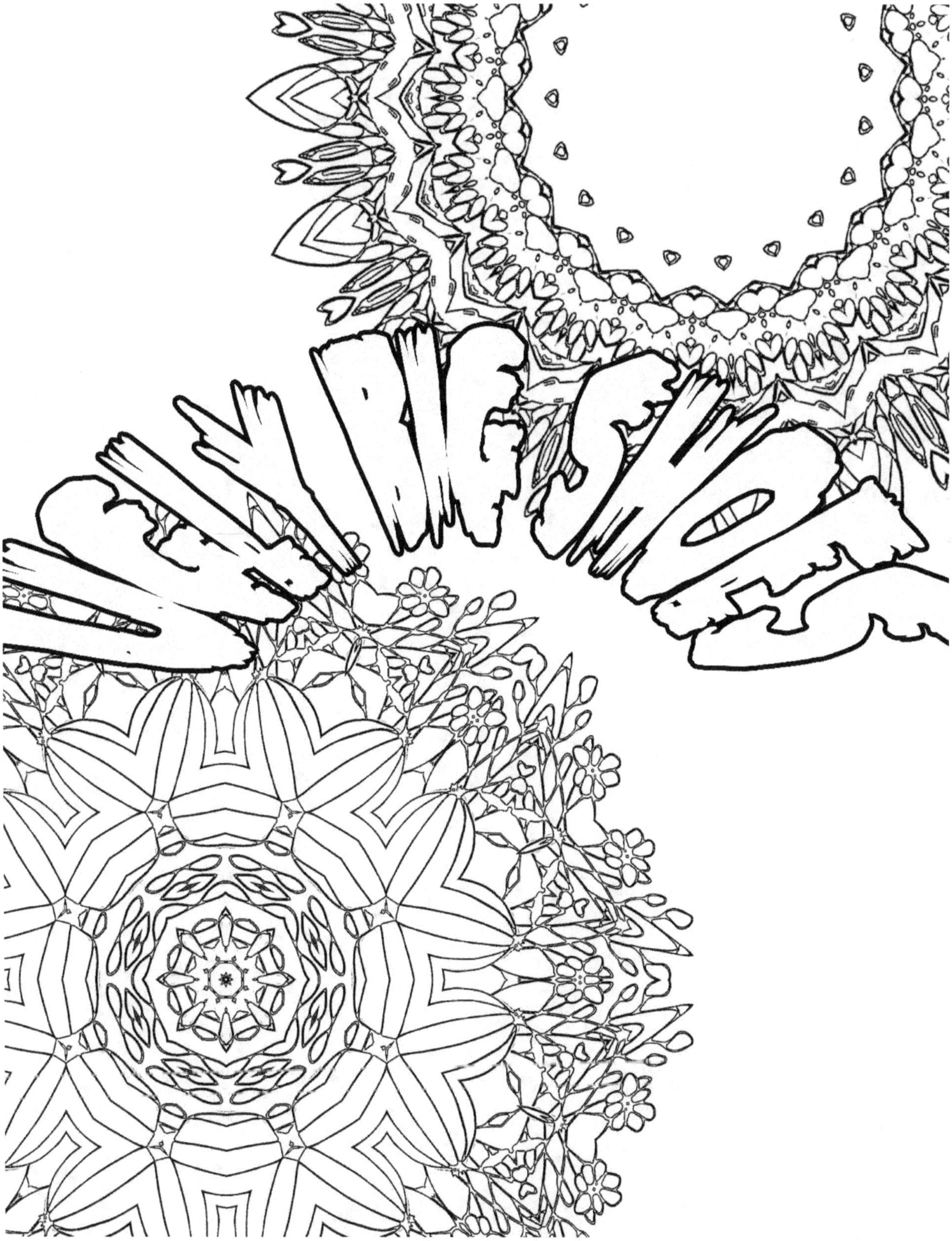
BIG SHOT

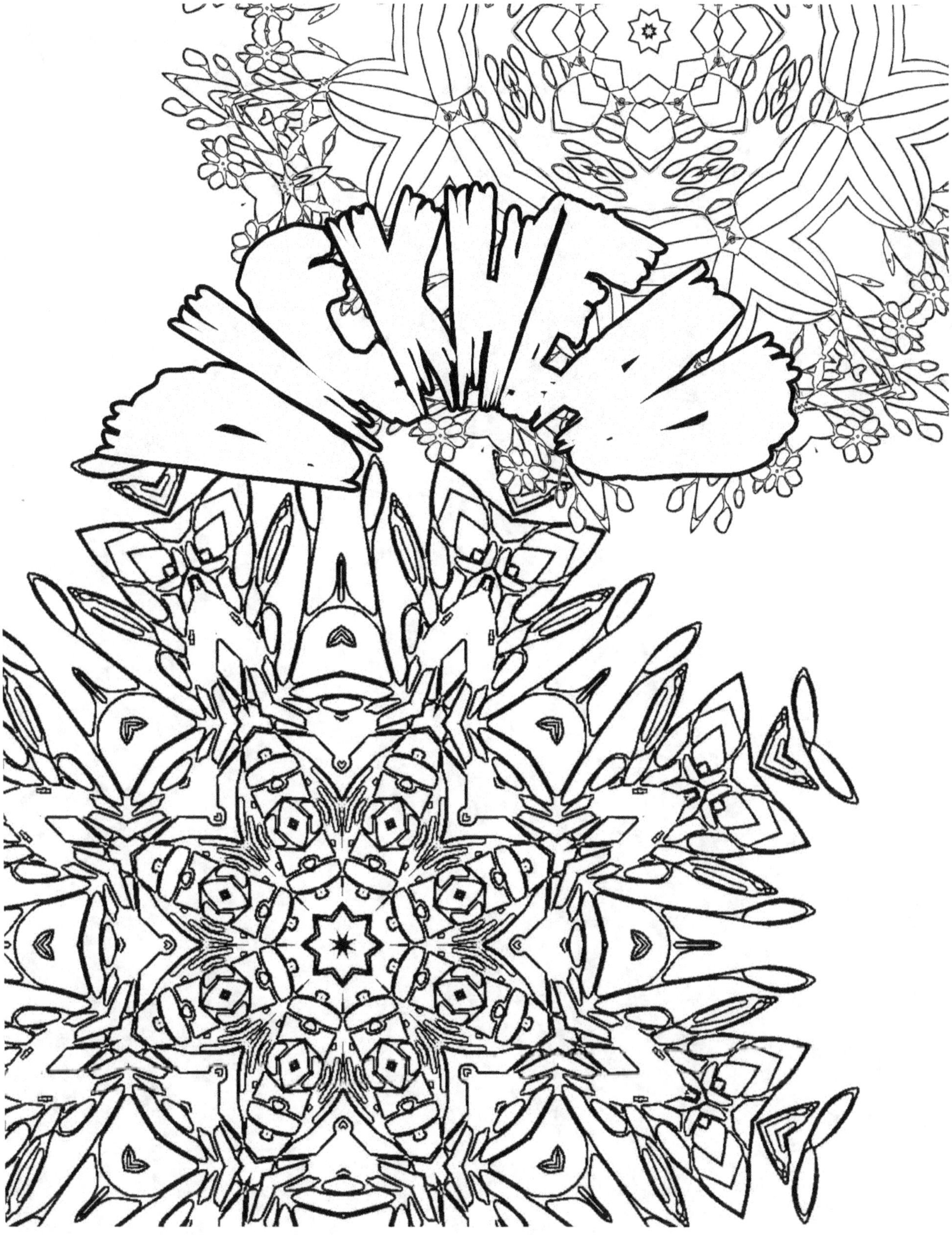

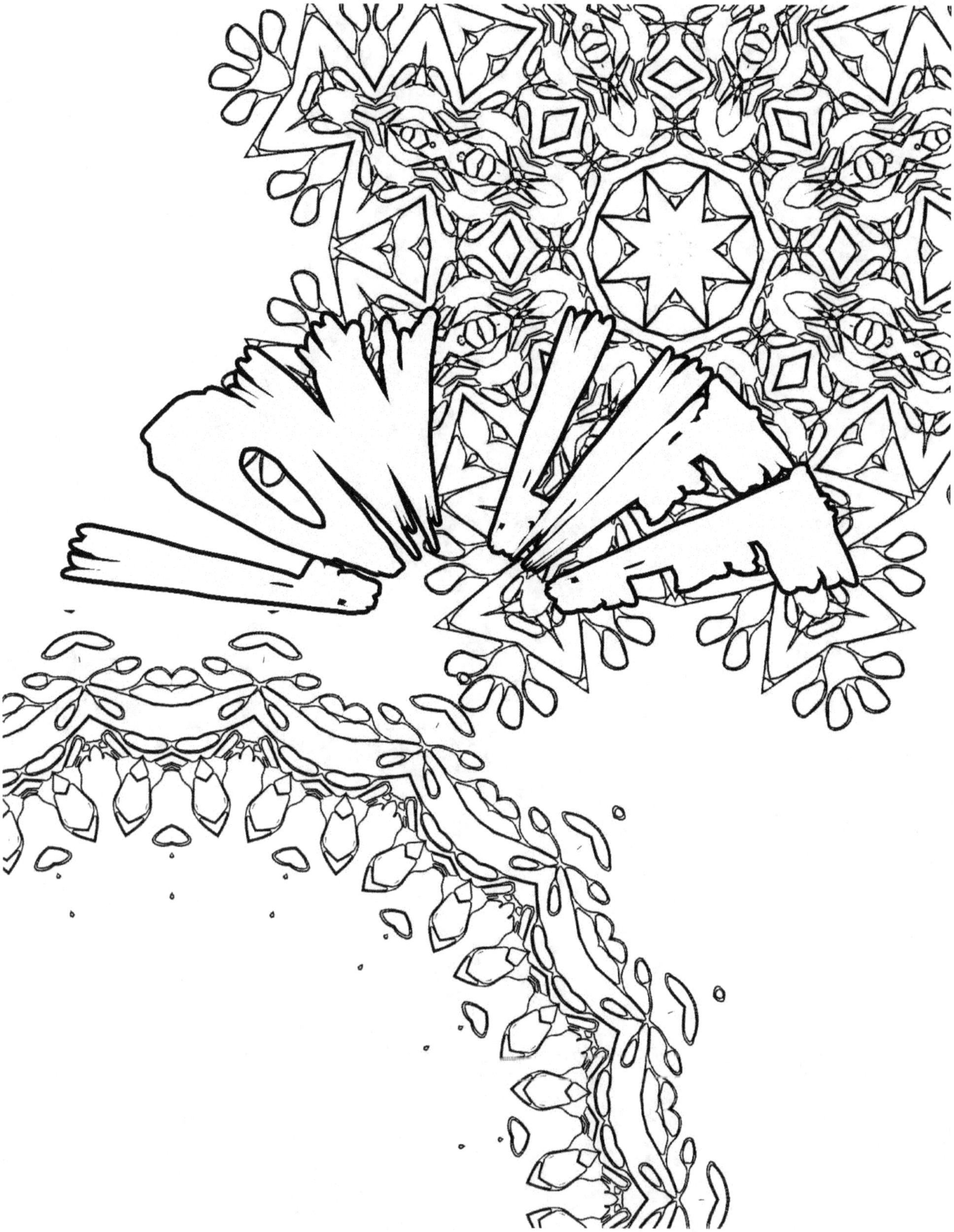

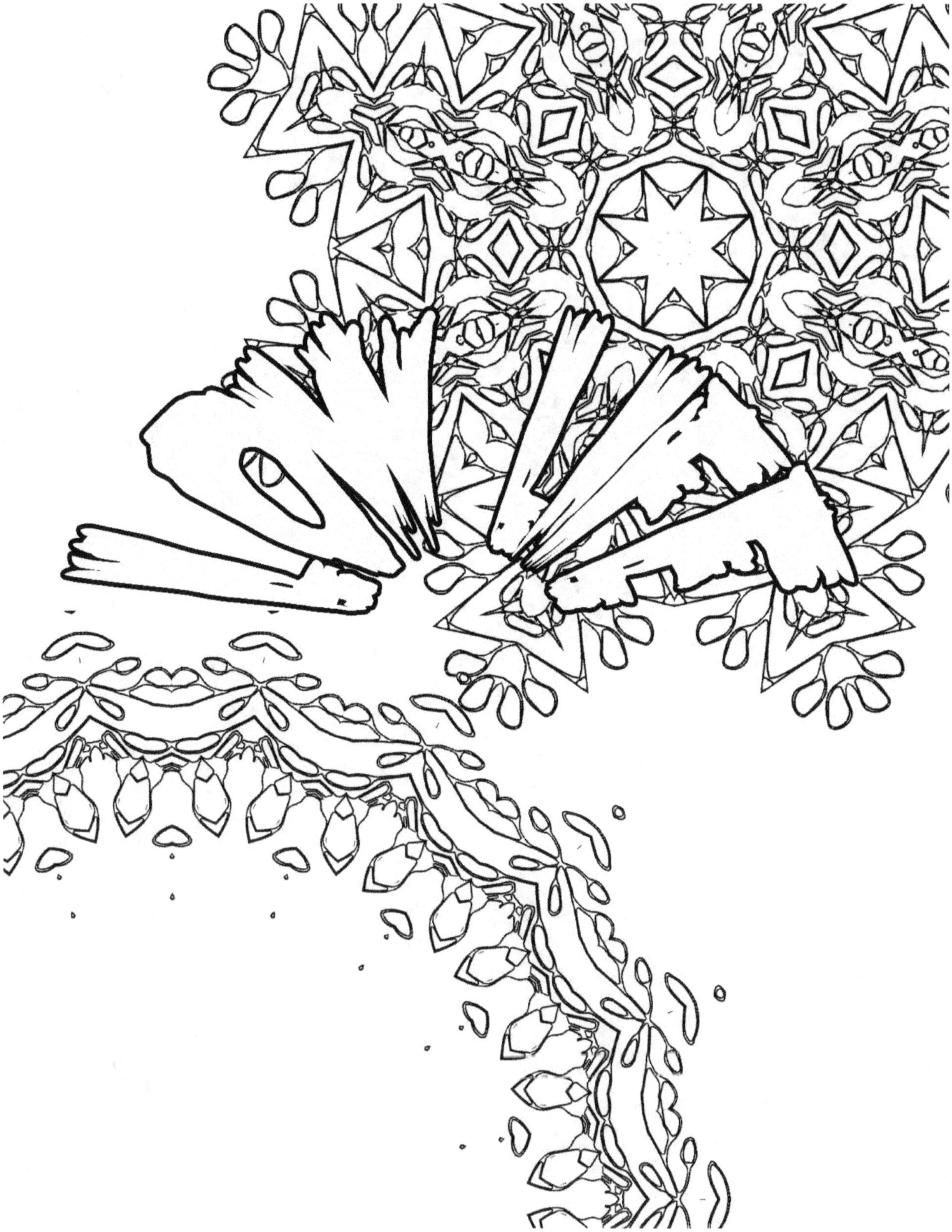

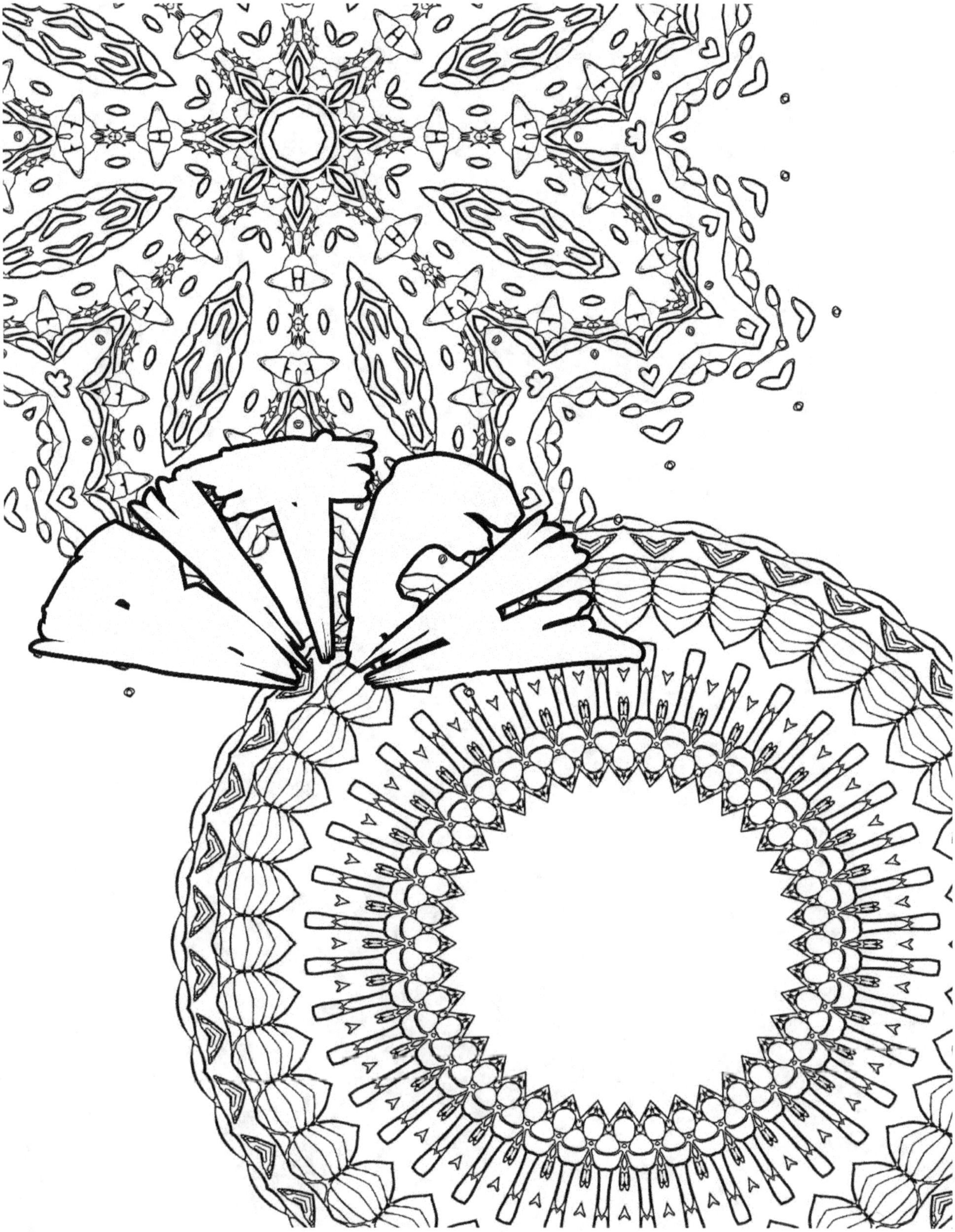

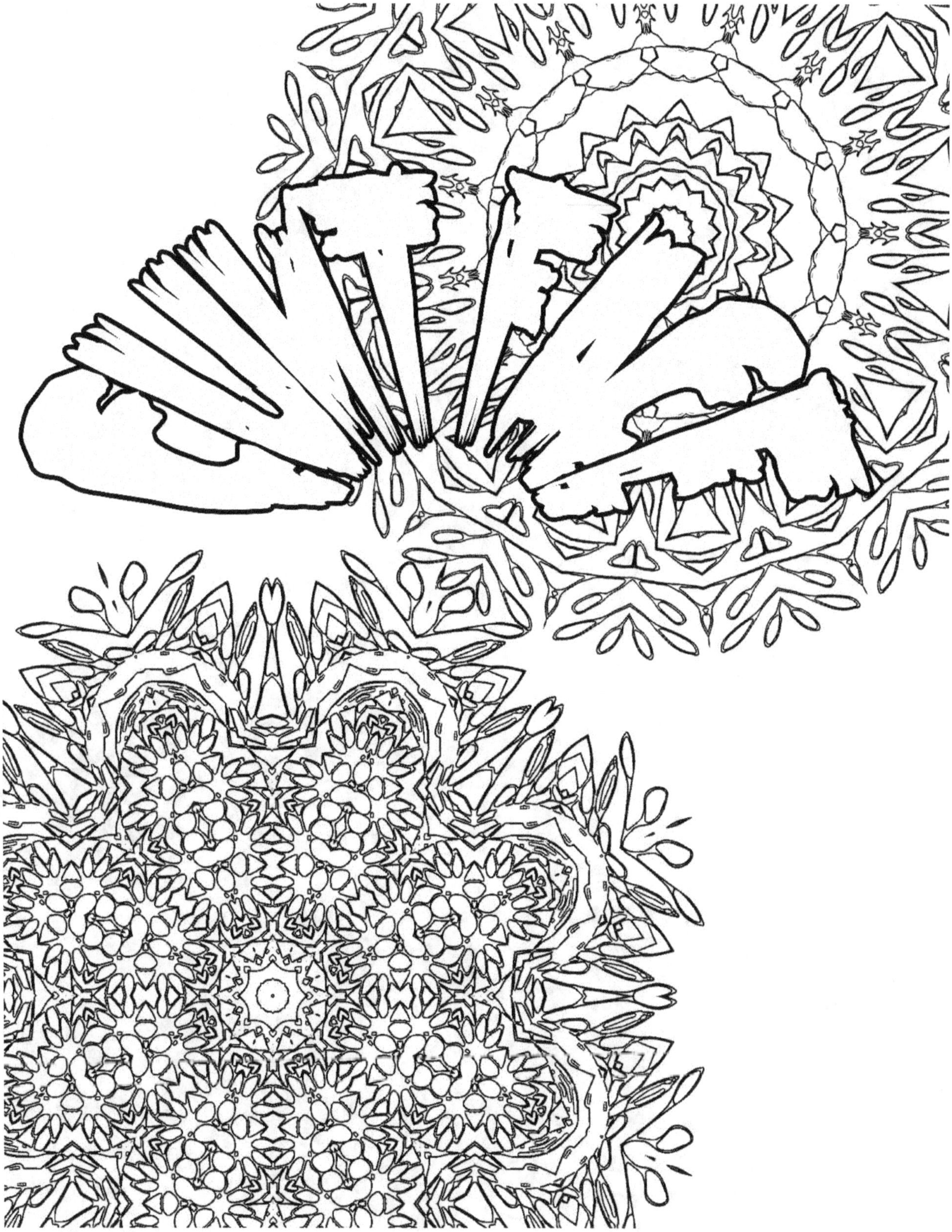

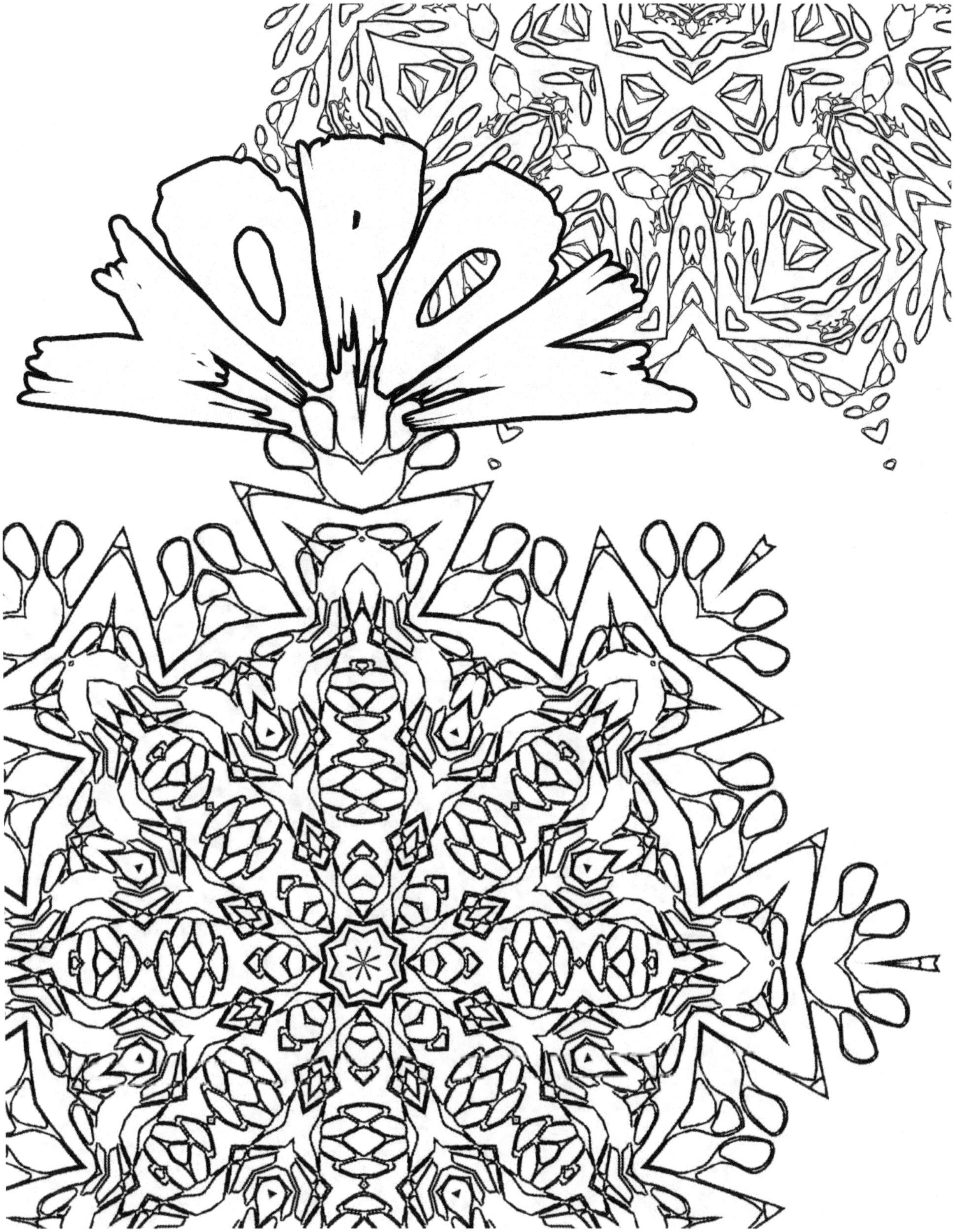

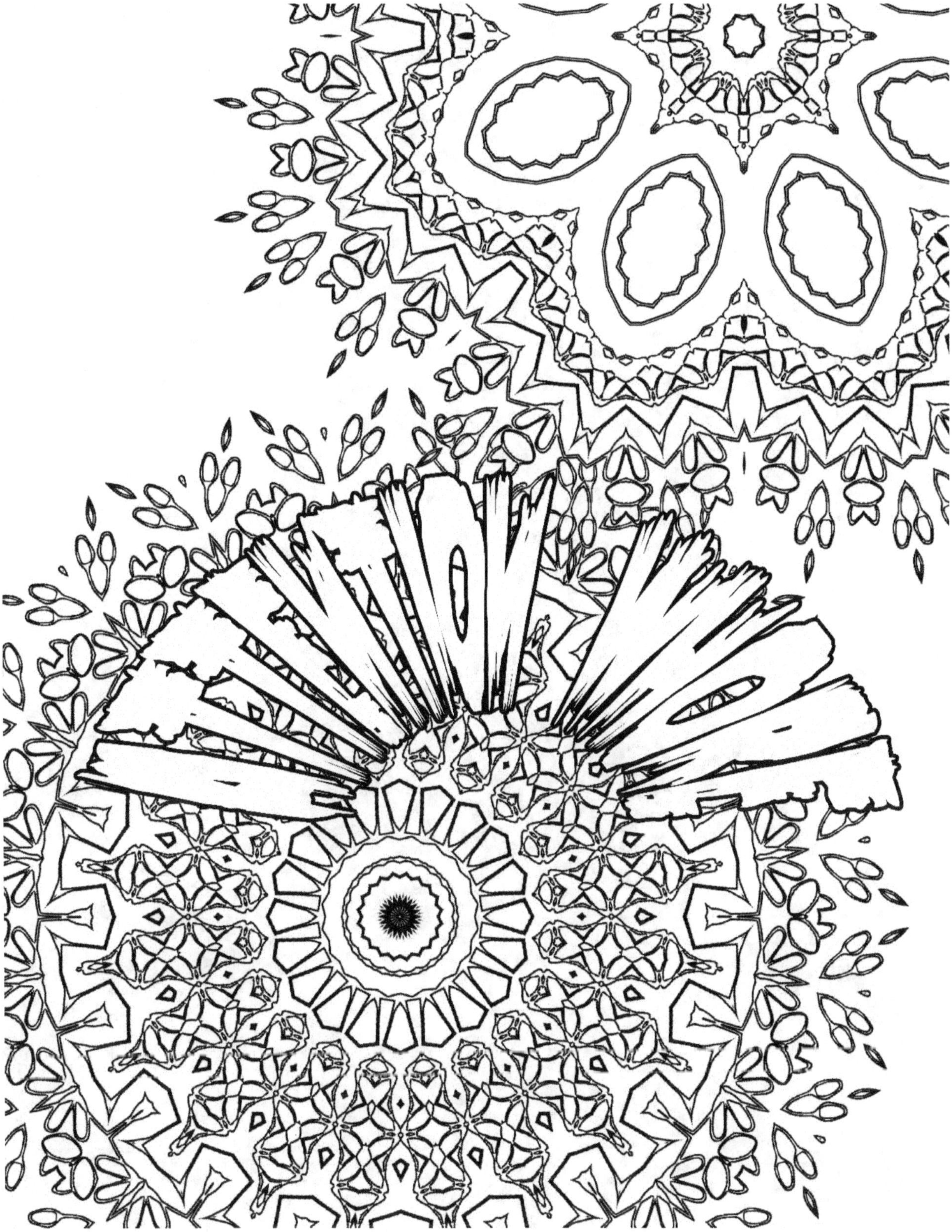

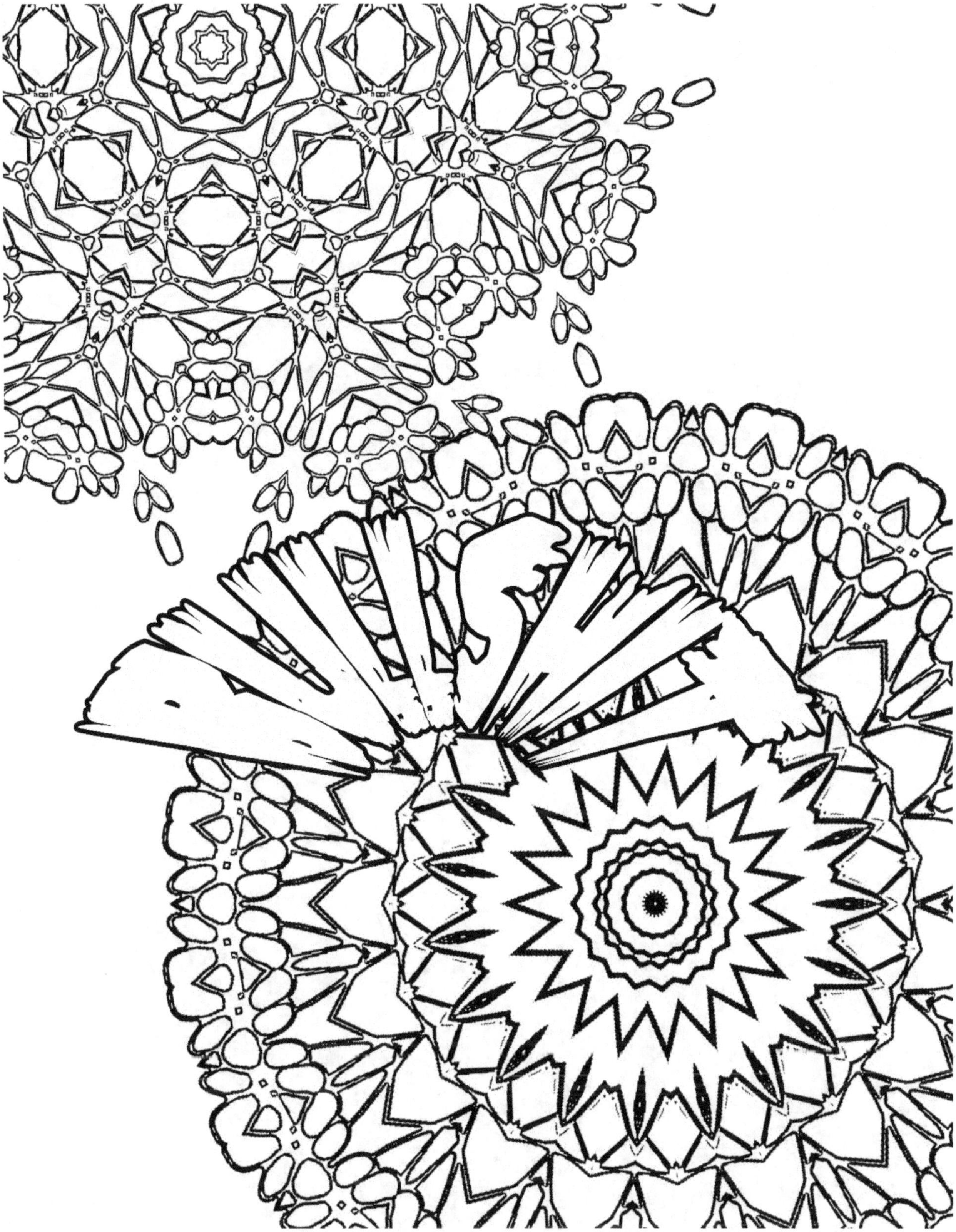

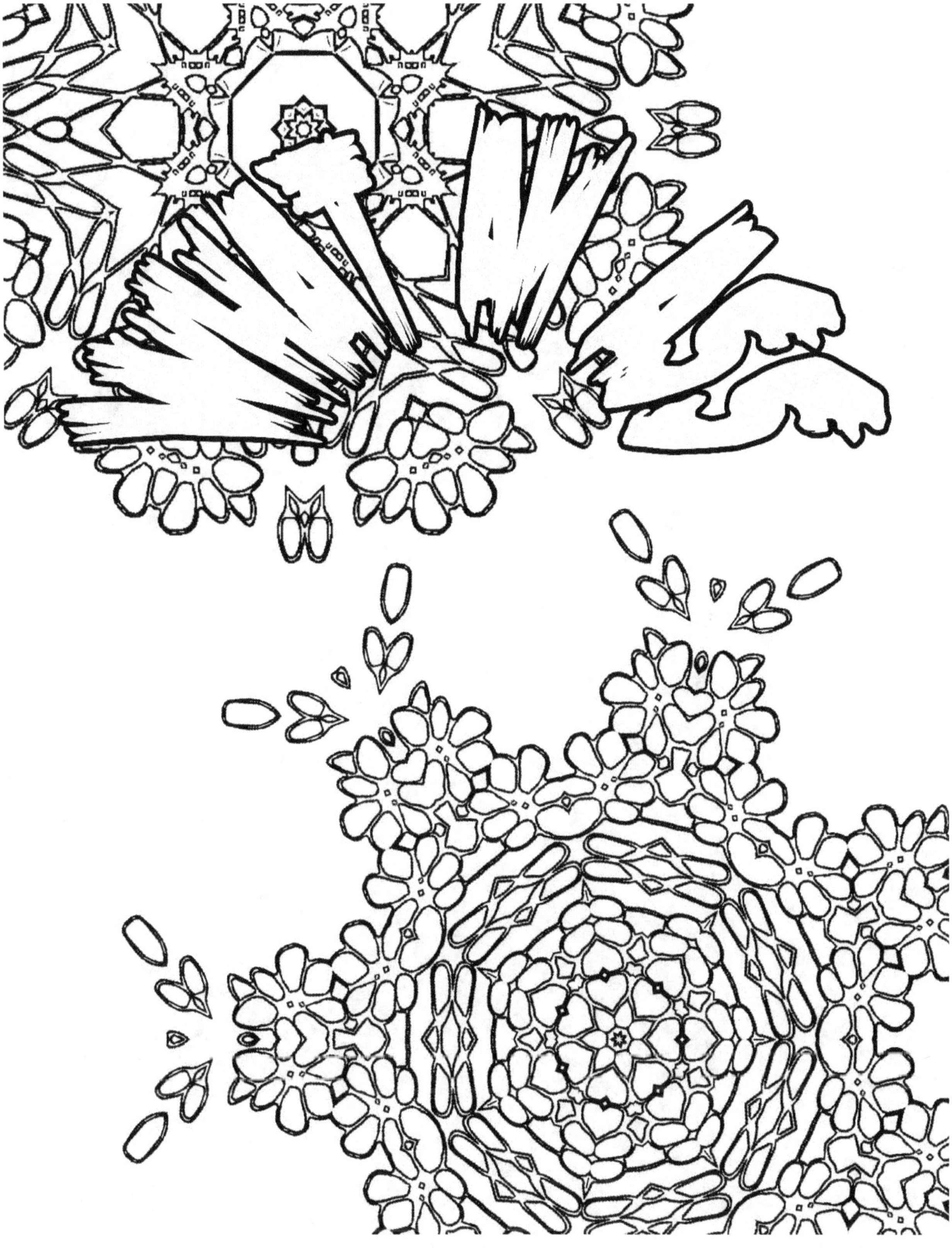

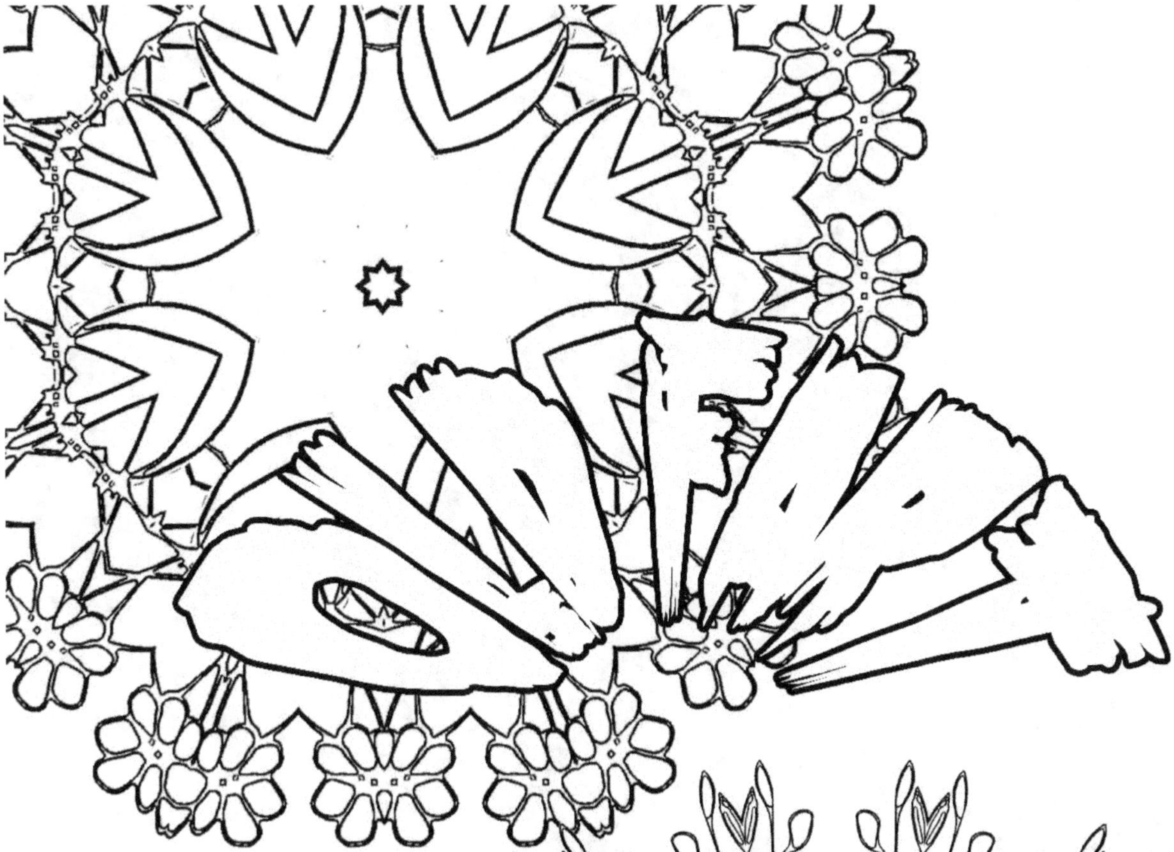

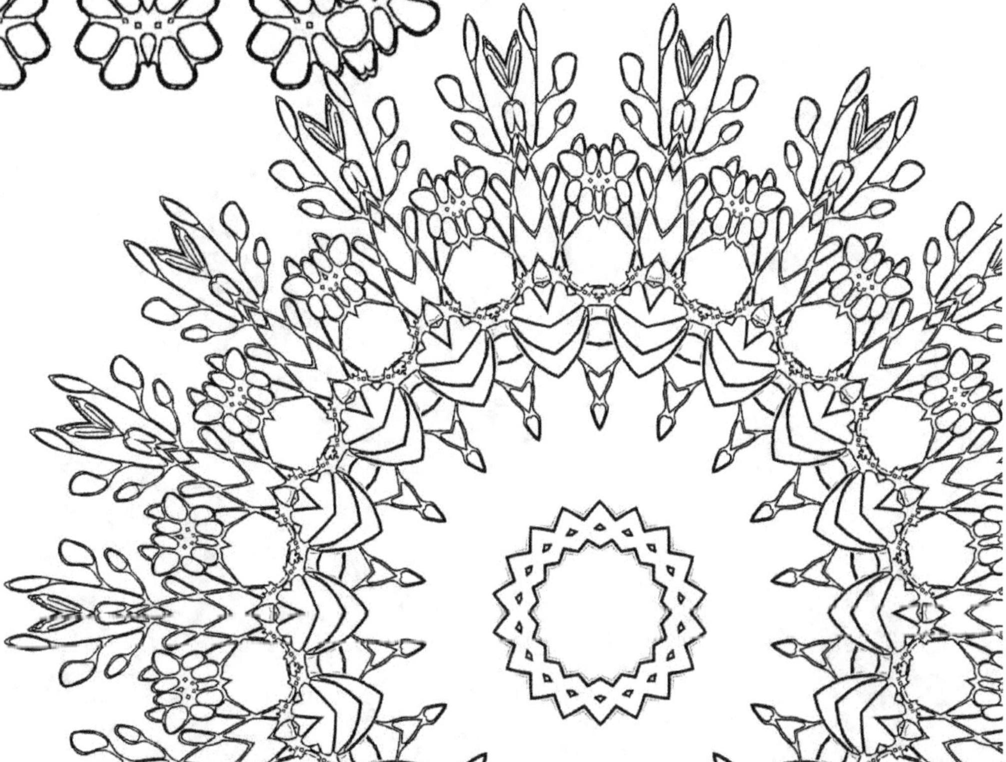

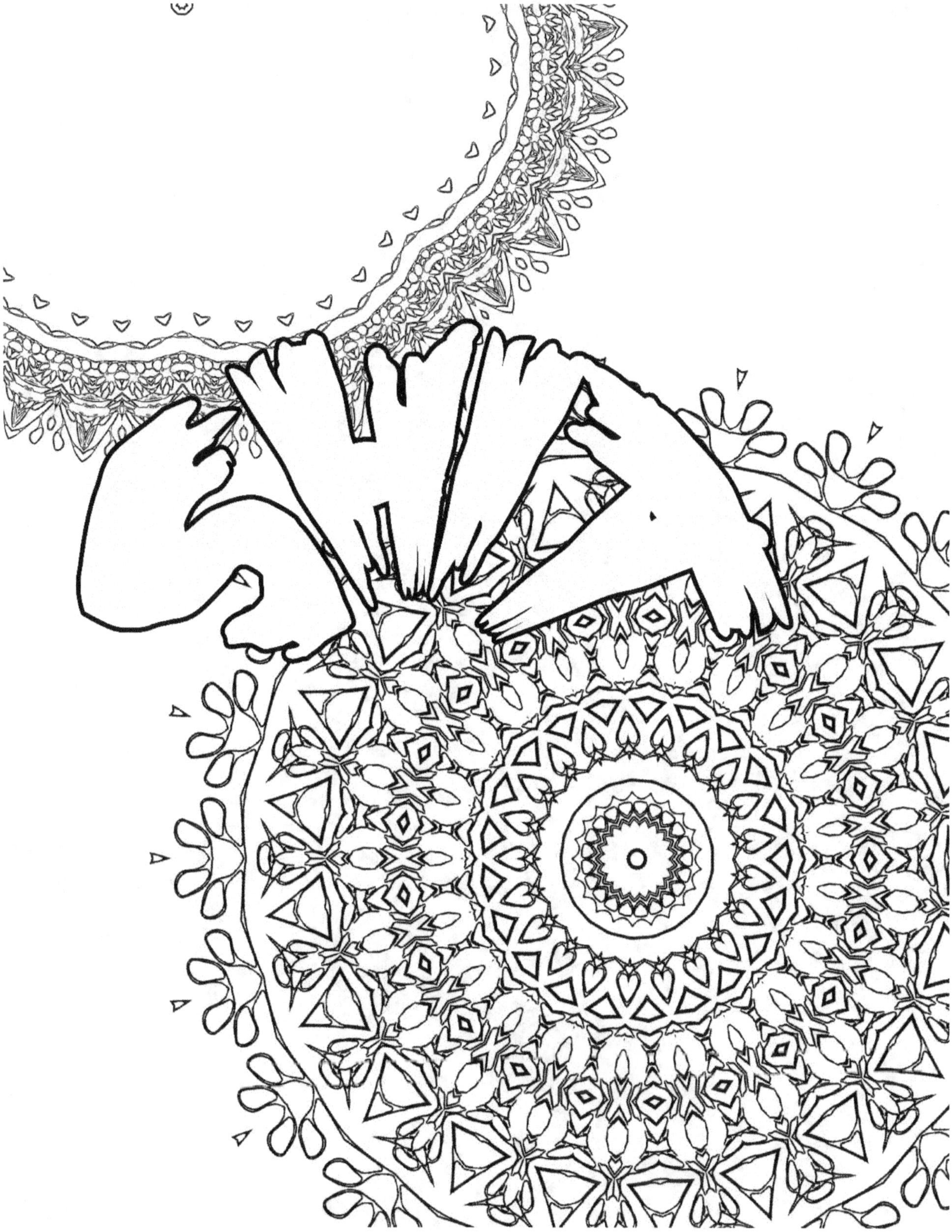

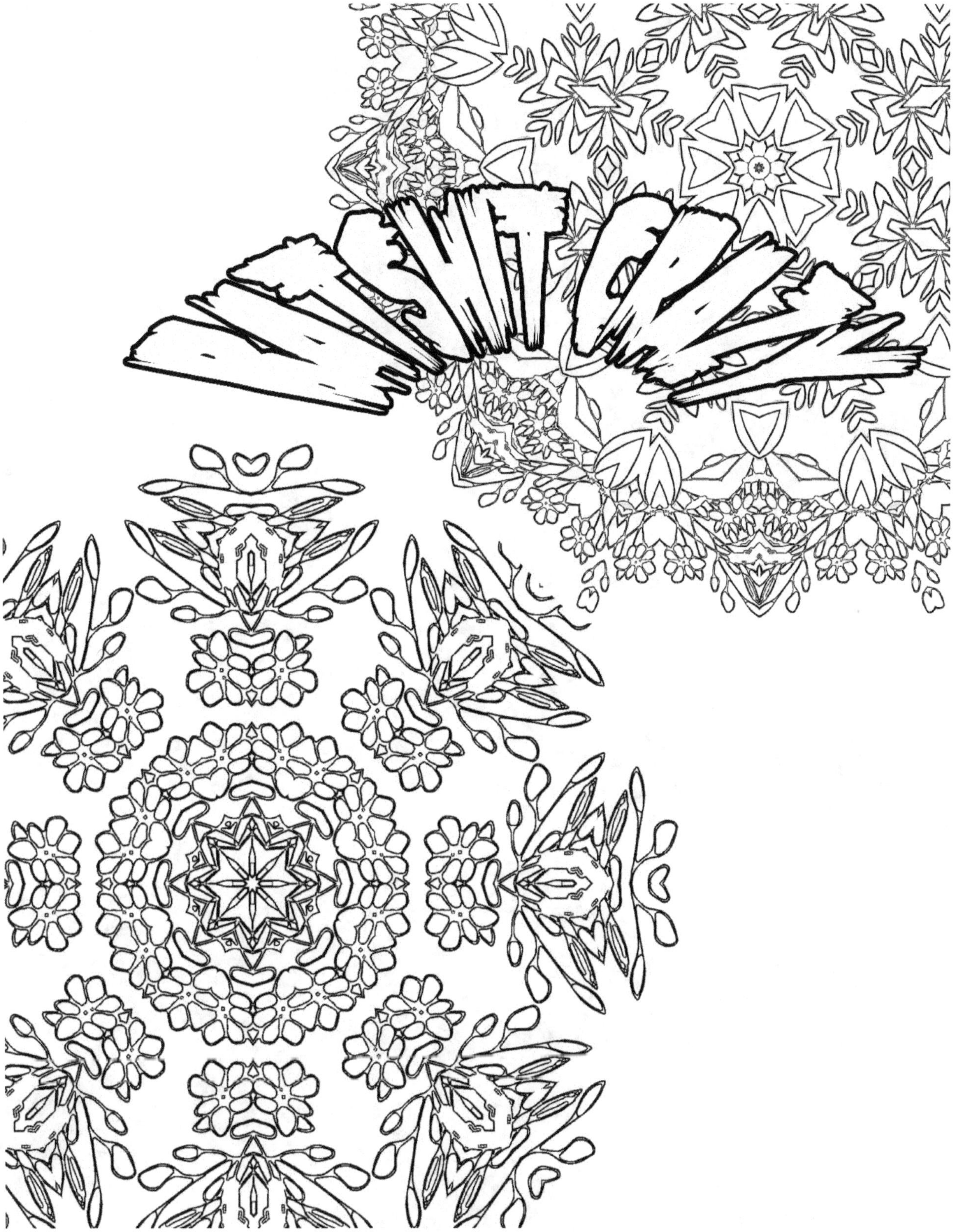

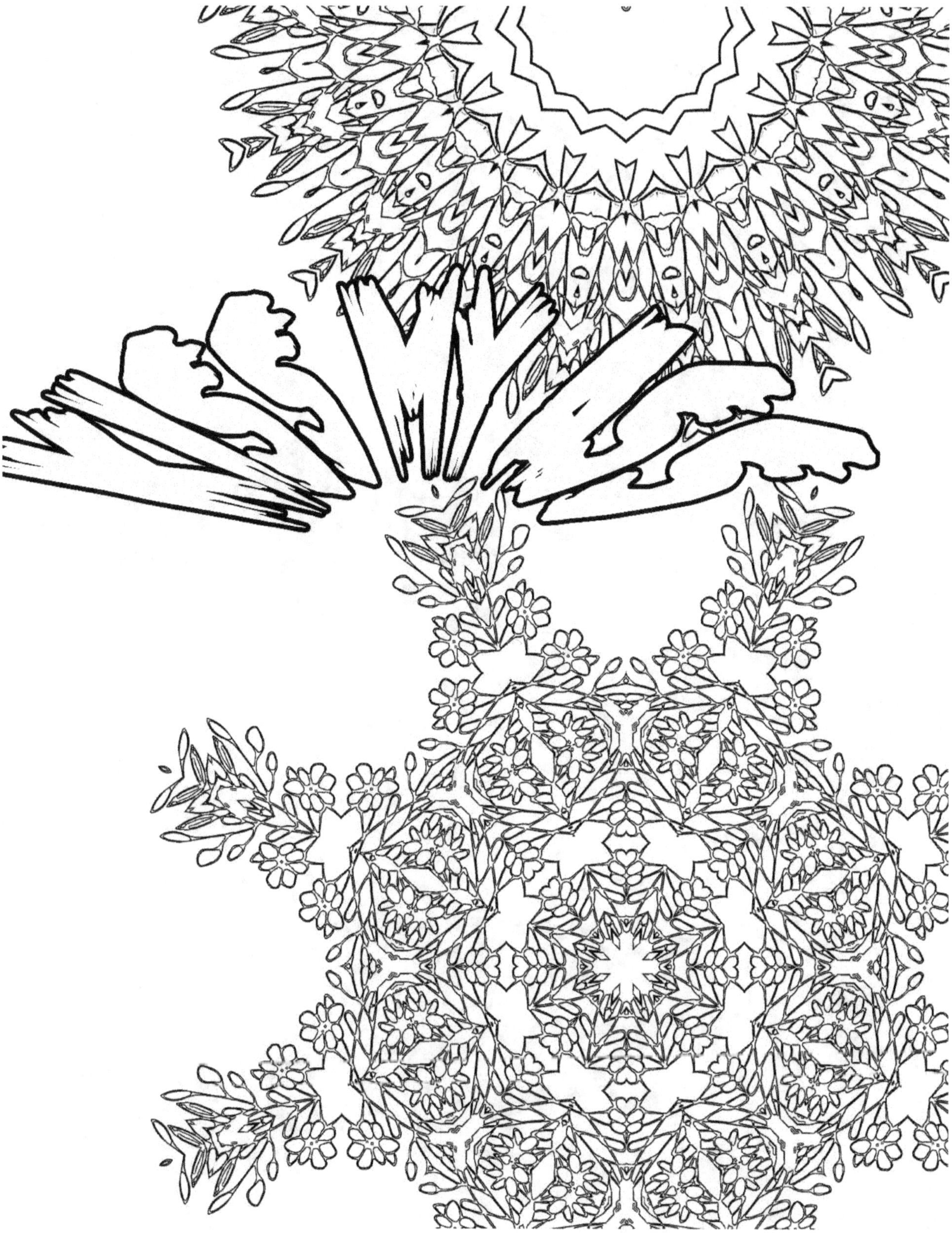

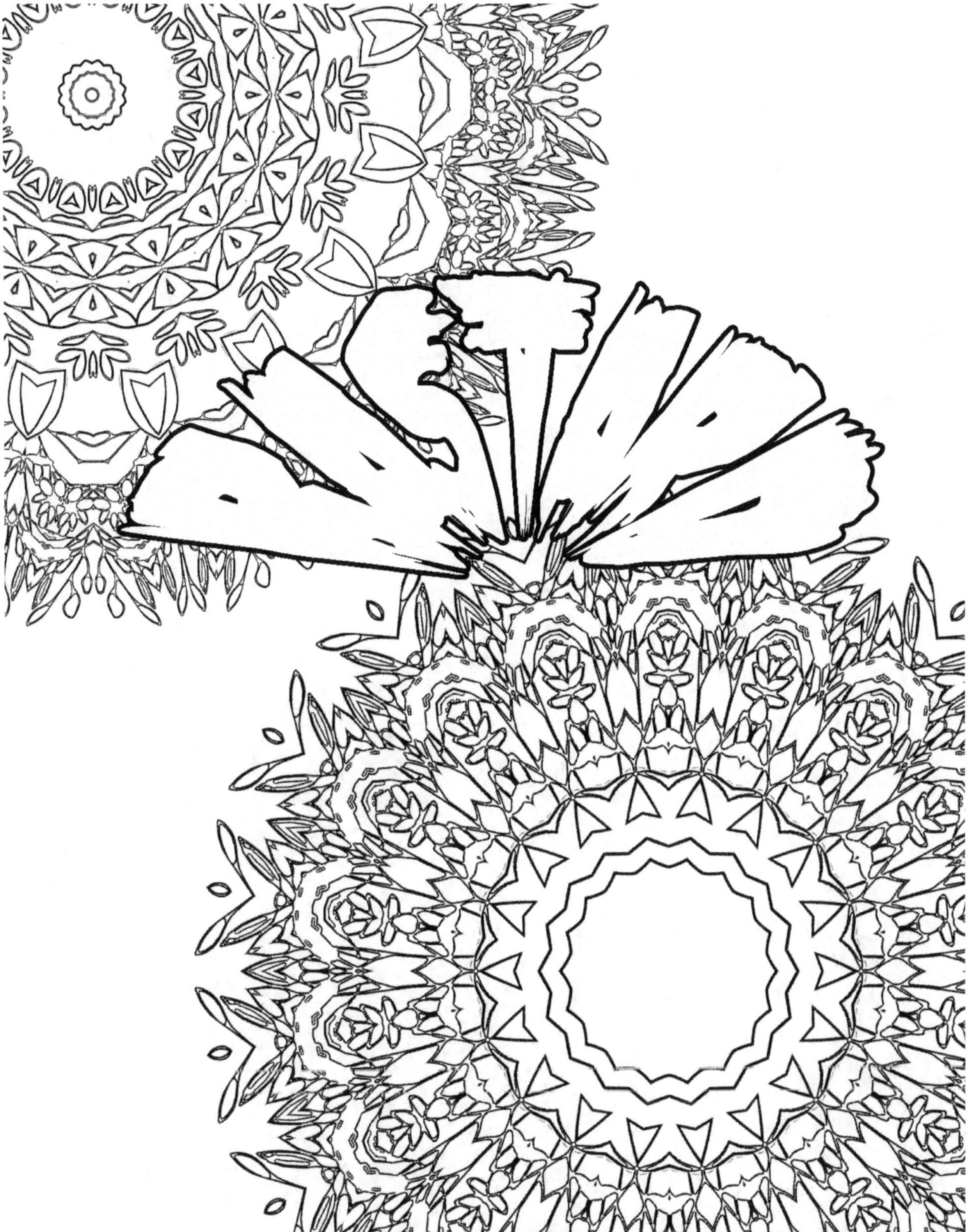

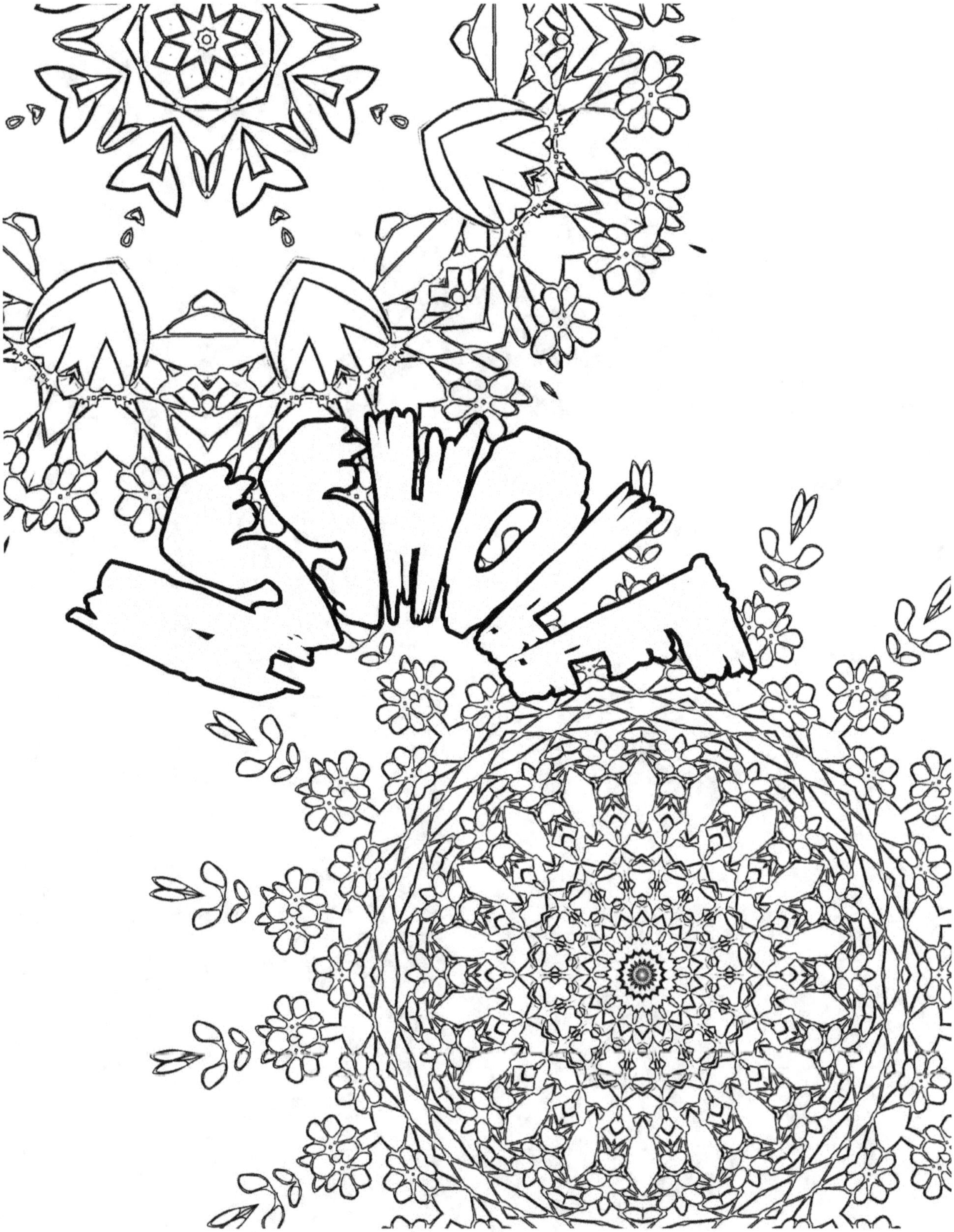

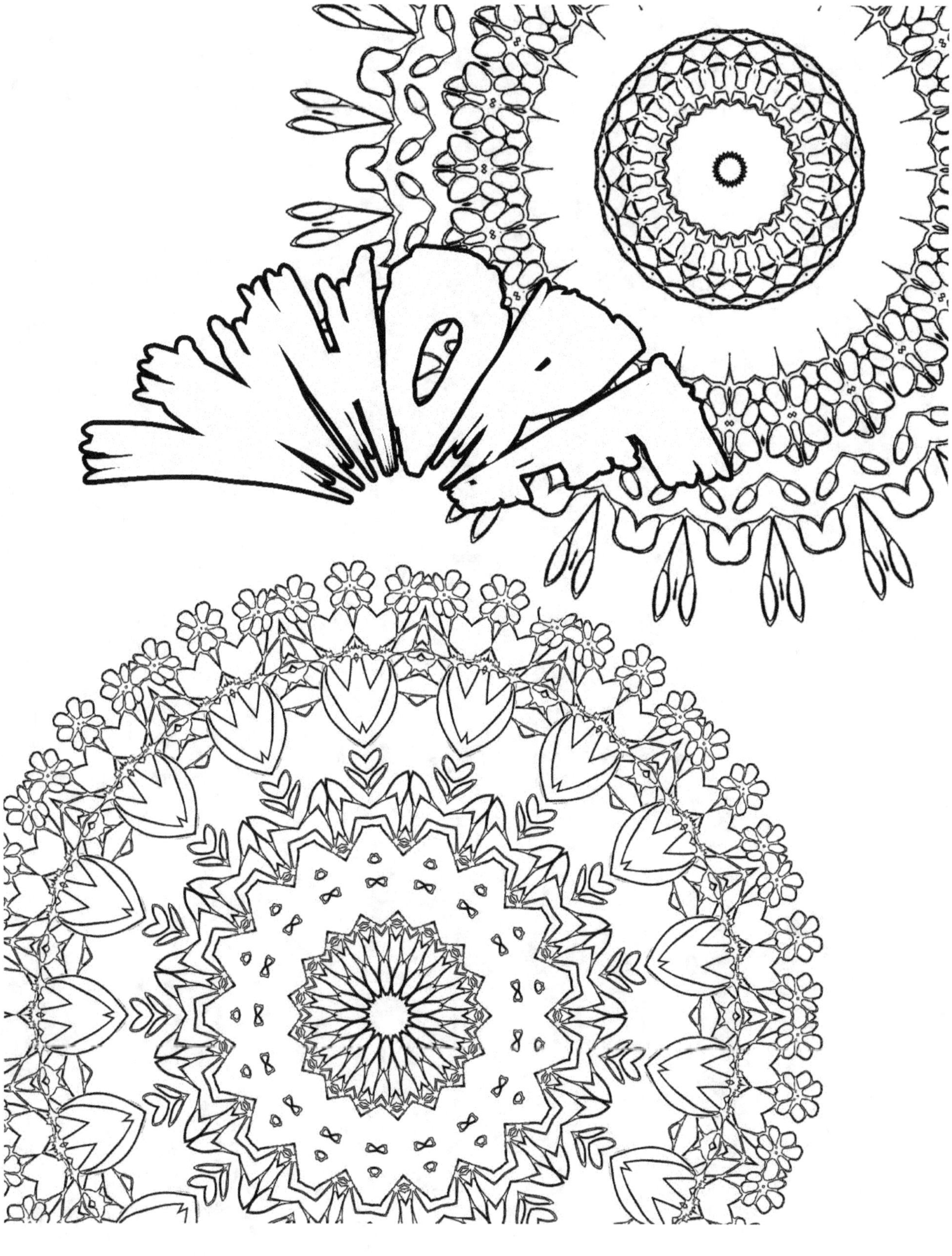

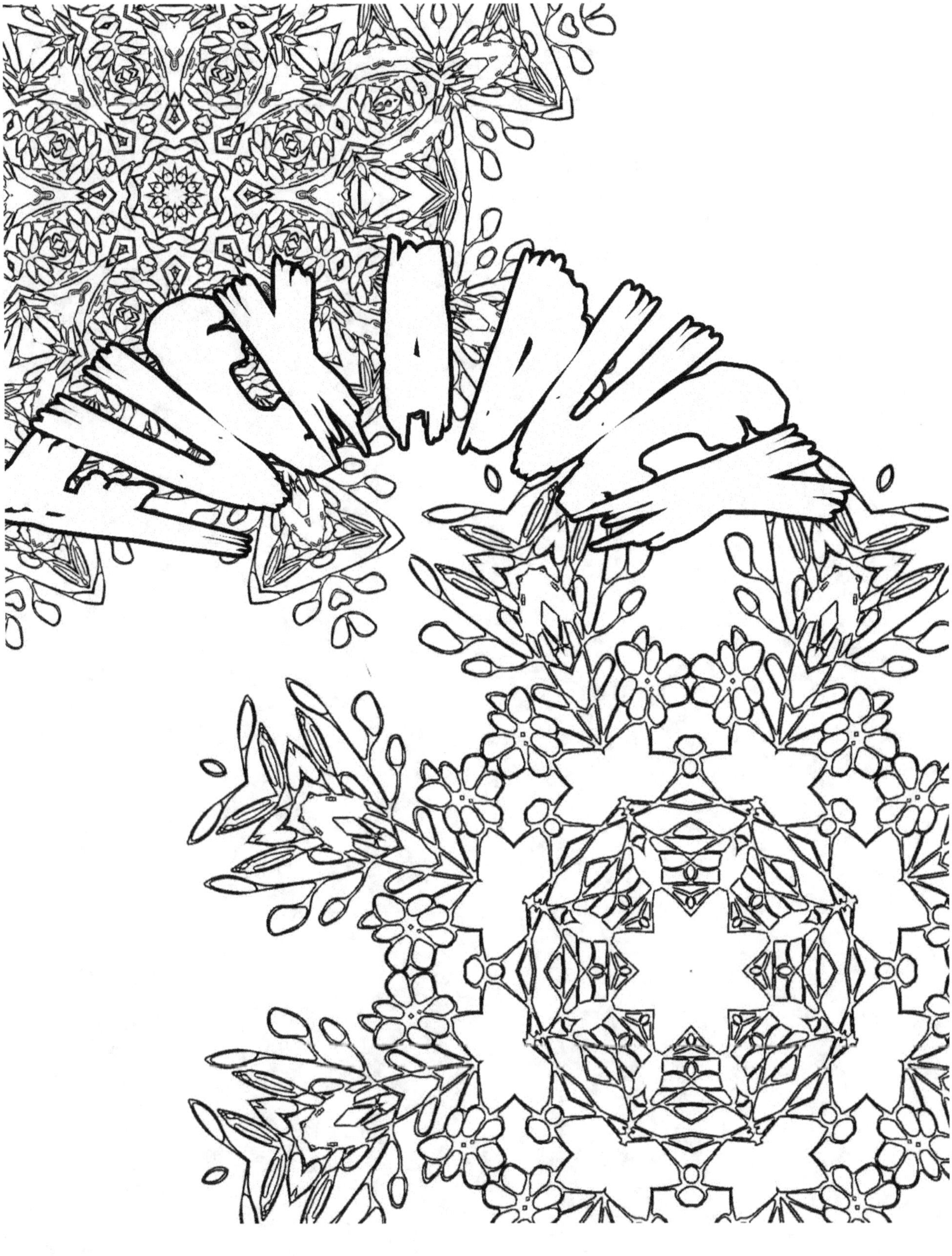

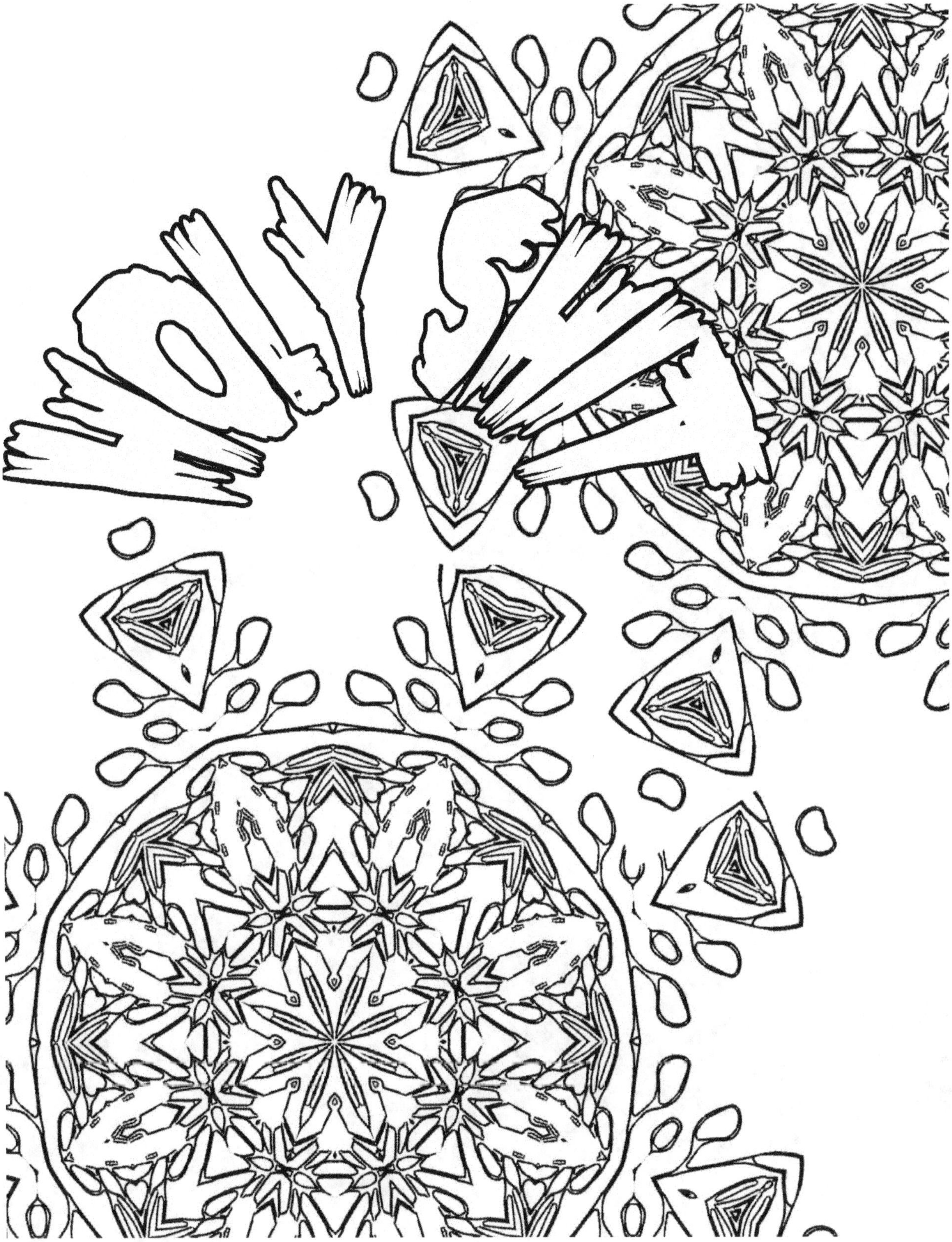
HOLY SHIT

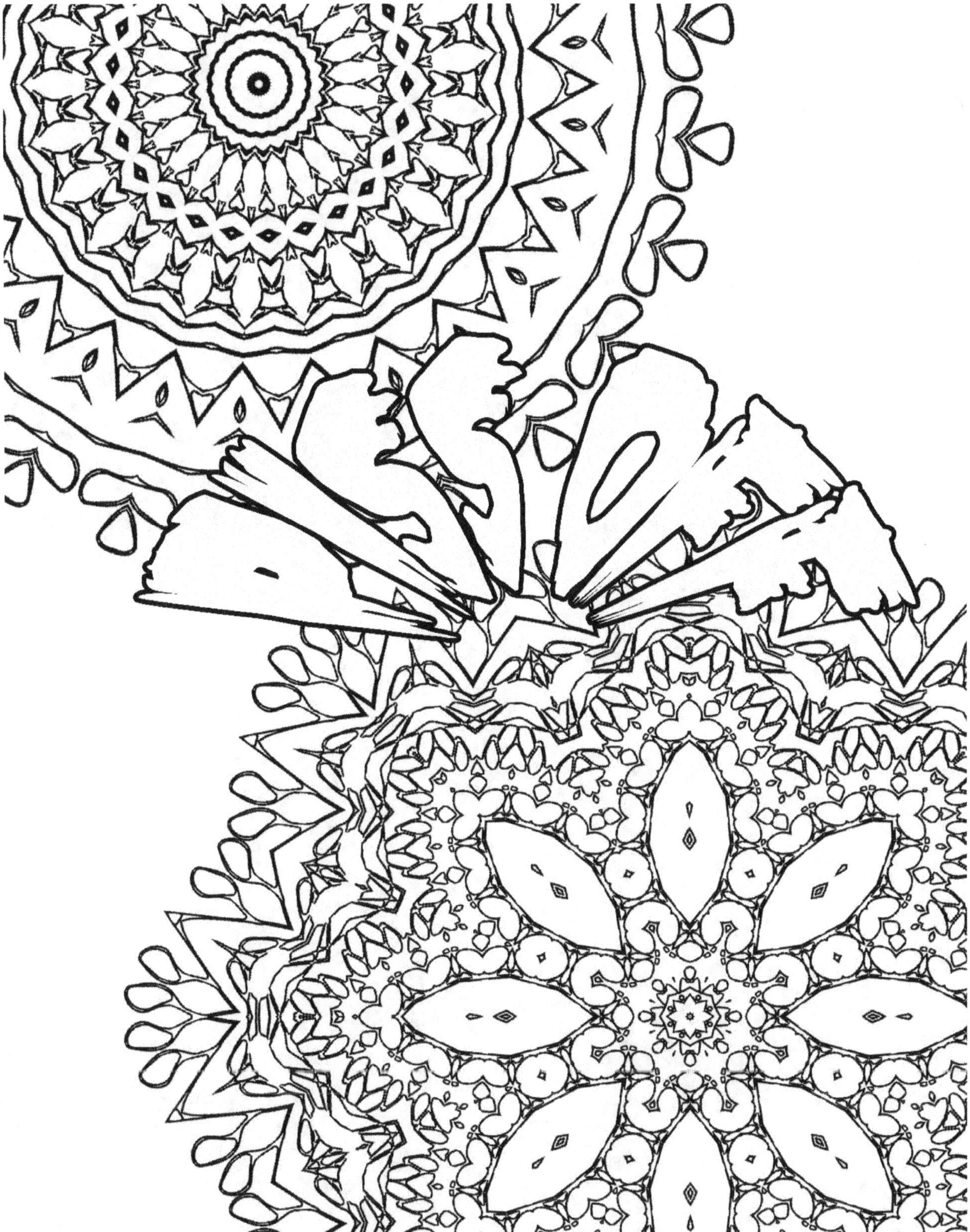

www.ingramcontent.com/pod-product-compliance
Lightning Source LLC
Chambersburg PA
CBHW081125180526
45170CB00008B/3009
* 9 7 8 1 5 4 4 8 3 3 4 9 1 *